Eliminating Sel[f-Defeating]
Behaviors in Children ana
the Child-at-Heart

To amy!

Thank you for all you do.
May all your goals and aspirations
be realized! Your friend,
(Linda Dianne Suda)

Linda Dianne Suda

Strategic Book Publishing
New York, New York

Strategic Book Publishing
An imprint of Writers Literary & Publishing Services, Inc.
845 Third Avenue, 6th Floor — #6016
New York, NY 10022
www.StrategicBookPublishing.com

ISBN: 978-1-60693-974-1
SKU: 1-60693-974-2

Printed in the United States of America

I dedicate this book to my daughter, Edna Louise Suda, for her loving support, encouragement, and the pressure she exerted to get me to write this book.

Contents

Acknowledgments

I want to acknowledge Daniel Solen, for the artwork on the cover and the certificate, CARMAGRAY Photography for the photo on the cover, and Dr. Jonathon Chamberlain, who first taught me about eliminating self-defeating behaviors and gave permission to use some of the stories he had used in his university classes.

In addition, I acknowledge those friends who gave their support, friendship, example, encouragement, and/or pressure to write my book, including; Marie-Louise Griffith, Amanda Holbrook, David and Connie Williams, Chris Sedler, Kristen Oaks, Patty Guntz, John and Janet Garrett, cousins Ken and Linda Solen, and all the professors including Mike Maughan and Richard Wootton, who told me I should write. Not to be forgotten are all the children who created a need for this program, which inspired me to produce it, and the Lord, who inspired me to create it.

Introduction and Background

When I worked as an elementary school counselor at a high-risk school, many more children needed help than I could see in the part-time position allotted to that school. I knew there had to be a way to help all the children who needed help, despite the overwhelming numbers. I remembered a mode of treatment that had worked on every patient I had used it on, and it could be done in a workshop format. The only problems were that not only was it for adults, but that it required a lot of journaling and abilities that normally come later in life. On my days off and after work, I redesigned the program so that it would be usable for children as young as six-years-old. What evolved was an easy-to-understand, fun program that, over the years, has worked for everyone who made an effort with it. Even adults indicated they preferred it to the traditional adult methods of eliminating self-defeating behaviors (ESDB). The children's version works as well as the adult version, but it is easier and often works faster. I always offer both versions to my clients who wish to eliminate a self-defeating behavior. I have yet to have anyone choose the adult version over the children's version.

When I first used it with children, it was presented in a few elementary school classrooms in six weekly sessions. I wore a gold sequined baseball cap, had gold foil pompoms, and lots of enthusiasm. At the end of the six weeks, I asked how many of the children had finished doing everything I asked them to do. Only a few in each classroom raised their hands. Discouraged, I asked how many had gotten rid of the self-defeating behaviors (SDBs) they were working on eliminating. All but one or two in each class raised their hands. I asked the ones who did not raise their hands what they thought had gone wrong, and every one of them said they had never tried. I asked those who raised their hands why they did not do all the assigned steps. Without fail, they said they had eliminated their SDB by the first or second step and started on another and then another. They said they first worked on something they wanted to change, as I had instructed, and then started working on things their teachers or parents wanted them to change. (Often, what they wanted to change first was the same as what their teachers and parents wanted changed.) In addition to the children's own accounts of success, teachers reported changes for the better in the children's behaviors, as well. The children asked for more garbage cans and other tools to assist in more behavior changes. They said they not only enjoyed the changes in their own behaviors, but also enjoyed knowing they had the power to change for the better. Many admitted to disobeying my instructions to work on only one SDB at a time and said they eliminated several SDBs at once.

Later I offered adults, even great-grandma-aged adults, the choice between the traditional adult version of the ESDB program and the children's version. They all chose the children's version, and, so far, I have yet to find anyone who *followed everything I told them to do,* who has not eliminated the behavior they chose to eliminate. Reports of success with the adult version of the ESDB program have been in the 90–98 percent range and thereabouts. The children's version is easy to understand and to follow, and the odds are excellent for success. I am including all the tools needed to succeed in this book. Without doubt, we choose whether we do our SDB or choose to behave as our Best Self.

First, I will go into some basics on thinking patterns. We all choose our thoughts, feelings, and behaviors. Many of you may disagree, but think about it. Suppose you step into an elevator and a man stepped on your foot and did not say something such as, "I am sorry." How would you feel? Would you feel angry? Now suppose you noticed the man was blind, had a prosthetic leg, and likely did not know he stepped on your foot; how would you feel? Your feelings would probably change. Would your behavior be different as well? Think: how would you behave before you knew he was blind and had a prosthetic leg? How would you behave differently once you knew that?

What happens to us does not determine our actions. It is how we think about what happens to us that determines our feelings, and our feelings determine our actions. Another example of how this works is camping. Most of my friends love camping. They look forward to it and go frequently. I, on the other hand, hate camping. I never go camping deliberately. Let's figure out what the difference is between my feelings and actions and those of my friends. Is the actual act of camping any different for me than for them? There is still a tent, a sleeping bag, a campfire, and the great outdoors—no matter which of us is camping. What actually is different? I asked some of them what they thought about when the word *camping* came to mind. They answered that when they think of camping, they think of beautiful scenery, getting away from everything, being with family, hiking, and fun. On the other hand, when I think of camping, I think of bugs and snakes, sleeping on hard ground, no controlled temperatures from central heating and air conditioning, no running water available close by, and toilets either nonexistent or far away. The thoughts my friends choose to have lead to pleasant feelings about camping, and those pleasant feelings about camping lead to behavior that leads to frequent camping. The thoughts I choose, however, lead to unpleasant feelings about camping, which leads to behavior where I never go camping unless forced to do so.

Two people going through the same trials and circumstances do not think, feel, or behave the same way. There are stories of people who grew up in slums and made good. There are also stories of some who grew up in wealthy circumstances who did not do well. It is not a matter of intelligence or opportunity alone; it is a matter of choosing your thoughts, which control your feelings, and your feelings control your actions.

Victor Frankl's experience during World War II is an excellent example of how we are in charge of our own attitude. While in a concentration camp that was far more horrible than any of us can imagine, and after losing his beloved wife and all that he had, he chose to think of others before himself, and even passed up a chance to escape at one point, in order to give others hope. Other prisoners in the same circumstance either gave up or turned against their fellow prisoners in order to survive. For some examples of how different attitudes in the same severe circumstances make a real difference, I highly recommend reading Victor Frankl's popular 1946 book, *Man's Search for Meaning*. Many editions are available.

Another example of thoughts controlling feelings that control behavior is a simple and silly incident that happened at my office not long ago. A man said something he meant as an insult to both my friends and me. He said, "You are so juvenile." (A few of us had been joking around at lunch.) I cheerfully thanked him. Another man said, "He meant that as an insult." I said, "I know, but I chose to take it as a compliment." The man who pointed out the insult laughed. Later, the man who originally intended the insult became a friend. What were my choices in that instance? I could choose to take the comment as an insult, I could choose to ignore him, or, on the other hand, I could choose to take what he said as a compliment.

If I had chosen to take his remark as an insult, how would I have felt? I would have likely chosen to feel angry. If I had chosen to feel angry, what types of behavior might I have chosen to exhibit? I might have chosen to say something angry in return, walked off in an angry huff, gossiped about it all over the building, or sat and brooded about it the rest of the day. My behaviors would then have provided examples for others in how to react, and the situation could have snowballed. Instead, my choice to see it as a compliment led someone else to choose to laugh and led me to choose to have a good attitude about it and to choose to have a good mood the rest of the day. My choice to continue to be friendly to the man who intended the insult led to a friendship with a man who others referred to at the time as grouchy and hot tempered. He exhibited friendlier traits, overall, after that incident.

This concept is important to understand: we choose what we think. What we think determines how we feel, and our feelings, in turn, determine our actions. What is it you are thinking? Can you think about it differently? What other options are there for ways to think about it? What other feelings would you choose if you thought about it in different ways? If you chose to feel in those different ways, how would your choice of actions or behaviors be different?

When I was in high school, my speech teacher, Mr. Keller, allowed me to try a fun experiment. I arranged for two of my friends to have a strong disagreement in class and "be sent to the principal" by the teacher. The entire event was scripted. Immediately following that incident, I was scheduled to speak. I pretended to be horrified at what happened—although I arranged all of it—and asked everyone to please write down exactly what happened and turn it in, so that the teacher, who came in shortly after the argument started, would know exactly what occurred. I said that the principal would likely want to know what happened from eyewitnesses. All of my classmates dutifully wrote down what happened from start to finish. They all appeared to be aghast at the terrible event. Nothing like that had ever occurred in that class before, and certainly not between two friends. I collected the descriptions and handed them to Mr. Keller. I then began my talk about perceptions. I gathered the descriptions back from Mr. Keller and read them to the class. It was amazing that, although an entire class had seen the incident, no two descriptions were alike. Many were quite different from each other. My two friends who had agreed to stage the argument came back into the classroom and were amazed. They calmly read the script I had previously given them, and the class sat in dead silence. I do not think one person in the class got either the wording or what happened correctly. Some of them took sides. Others expressed anger that the two disrupted class in this manner. The entire class understood my point about perceptions in the speech I gave that day.

Now, think for a minute, if everyone was watching the exact same thing happen at the same time and no one got what actually was said or how it happened, how many times could our own perceptions be wrong about what we see? Why are our perceptions wrong? We choose our thoughts about what we see, hear, and feel. It was interesting that the friends of one or the other actors saw their own friend as the one wronged. The class chose what they thought about what happened—subconsciously, yes, but they chose the thoughts. Because they chose those thoughts, they then chose their feelings based on those thoughts. Had this gone on farther, one can only imagine what might have happened in that high school environment.

If you think thoughts are automatic, think again. Remember the first time you drove a car. You had to think about getting the key, unlocking the door, opening the door, sitting down, putting on your seat belt, putting the key in the ignition, checking the mirrors, turning the ignition key, and so forth. Now, when you drive, what do you consciously think? *What route do I take? Where am I going?* Do you even think about whether you have to put the key in the ignition or put on your seatbelt? The thoughts are automatic—or are they? What is really happening is that you have created brain pathways that are shorter, and the thoughts remain below the level of your conscious thought. If we want to change our behaviors, we need to stop, catch ourselves as early as we can in the thought process, and change our thoughts. We need to go back to when we first learned the behavior, and then change each thought. The first time you made your favorite food, or used a computer, you had to stop and think about each step. Now, you just do it. If you wanted to change the recipe, or updates were made to the computer or program, you would need to stop and think about what you were doing, again. If you want to change behaviors, you need to stop and think. This program helps you do that.

Have you ever said, "He made me angry" or "She forced me to do it"? How did the person you blamed for the feelings or behaviors get so much power over you? If someone were to slash the tires on a new car that I just brought home from the dealer and then beat the car with a sledgehammer and laugh, who is responsible for my feelings or behavior? Is the other person so powerful that they control my own feelings and actions? Can he force me to be angry, punch him, or take other revenge? If so, how did he get that power? Does he have a magic wand? Does he control wires in my brain to make me react certain ways?

Thinking about this same example, I actually have a choice in how I think, feel, and behave. I can choose to think, *That person is obviously not in his right mind and needs help. I wonder what I can do to get him that help or assistance.* I would also be thinking, in such a situation, that the car is only an object and is not as important as that person who just destroyed it. My actions might include praying for the person, doing what I could to get him evaluated for psychological issues or treated with medications, telling him I forgive him, and offering kindness. (I most likely would notify the authorities, but it would not be to get revenge. I know people who have had experiences similar to this. Some did not even notify the authorities, but took the vandal under their wings.) My thoughts could also be something like, *That horrible person just destroyed my new car! I am not letting him get away with this.* In that case, my feelings would be anger, hurt, and pain. My actions could be anything from nursing my anger and hurt for many years and letting it fester

and destroy me, to physically attacking the person and screaming at him, harassing him or his family, badgering the courts to
punish him to the maximum and trying to ruin him and his family financially. The only power the person actually had was to
destroy my property. He did not have the power to force me to
be angry against my will, nor to act in an angry fashion against
my will. The choice in how to think, feel, and act was still mine.
I act, not re-act. If I punch him, it is because I chose to punch
him. If I show kindness in return, it is because I chose to do so.

Another example to consider might be if someone
approached me and said something judgmental and unkind to
me. Does she have the power to make me angry and respond in
an angry fashion? No, she does not. How I react depends on my
choice of thoughts and feelings, and, based on those, how I
choose to act. What are my choices in how I think? *That poor
woman is obviously misinformed. That biddy, what right does
she have to stick her nose in my business? That poor woman
must have very low self-esteem to be saying something so judgmental and unkind. She needs love.* Depending on my thoughts,
my feelings could be anger, pity, love, or even gratitude for
pointing out that I might have a problem. My actions, depending on the feelings and thoughts I chose, could be as different as
screaming at her, telling her how stupid she is, thanking her for
her concern, simply explaining reality in a calm voice, telling
her I like her hairdo, or any number of other reactions. The
judgmental woman does not have the power to force me to
think, feel, or act in any particular way. I can choose to stew
over the statement, do something kind for her, gossip about her,

tell her how stupid something she does appears, or forget she ever said anything.

Along this same line, a person who grows up in an abusive home does not have to choose to abuse others or turn to drugs or alcohol. They choose their thoughts about what happened. Their thoughts determine their feelings, which determine their actions. I know of several very good people who were abused as children or who grew up in an alcoholic home. They chose to do something good with their lives and have different thoughts than those who chose to abuse others and nurse their anger, or those who turned to chemicals to forget their pain. It is not what happens to you, it is what you think about what happens to you. Then the thoughts determine the feelings, which determine your actions.

What kinds of behaviors are self-defeating? The answer is simple—any behavior, thought, or feeling that stops you from being your best self. It could be biting your nails, anxiety, depression, stealing, gossiping, anger management issues, addictions, excessive spending, laziness, overeating, and many other issues. Keep in mind that some problems, such as depression and anxiety, may have a biological basis and, thus, may require medications. (If you have suicidal thoughts, be certain to get professional help immediately; if you have more than a passing thought of suicide and have a plan or the actual intent to follow through with it, go to your nearest emergency room immediately.)

One question: how hard is it to change? The answer: if a six-year-old can do it, do you think you can? Children who are six-years-old and up have used this program successfully to change self-defeating behaviors.

I still remember the excitement of a fourth-grade student who conquered the SDB of nail biting, and another who conquered the SDB of getting into fights. No one ordered them to fix those SDBs. They wanted to do it. When they eliminated those SDBs, they started working on others. Students came to my office asking for more garbage cans or price tags, because they eliminated another SDB and wanted to work on still another. No one asked them to do it. They wanted to change. (They usually did not listen to my admonition to work on one at a time, and many worked on multiple SDBs at once and eliminated all of them. I do not recommend this at all.) What I found was that, although my instructions were to work on an SDB they themselves wanted to eliminate (not something they were told to change), the SDBs they worked on either first or second were those that their parents or teachers wanted them to eliminate. They were eliminating them because they themselves wanted to eliminate them, not because someone told them to do so. If anyone thinks children enjoy performing self-defeating behaviors, I beg to differ. The children expressed pleasure at being empowered to change their own behaviors and feelings.

When working with adults using the children's version, it was rare that anyone needed assistance beyond the second or third step. Upon follow-up questioning, the reports were that the SDBs had been eliminated earlier than the final step.

In using the ESDB program for adults, I remember one client from years ago who just wanted to stop biting her fingernails. She said she had never dated. I noted she was not caring for her appearance. After a couple of sessions, she reported she was now caring for her nails. I noted she was now wearing clothes that were more stylish, now had a becoming haircut, and was wearing makeup as well. At the next session, she reported she was dating. She did not show up for any more sessions, and I wondered what happened. I ran into her on campus a while later, and she was exuberant! She showed me her well-manicured and beautiful nails, as well as a beautiful engagement ring. She said she had not come back because she not only eliminated her SDB, but also was now happy and engaged to be married.

Another client who tried the ESDB program was in danger of losing her children and her husband. She had a long history of neglecting her children and housework, and her husband reported he was tired of having his shoes stick to the dirty kitchen floor as he walked across it. The court had ordered her to psychological treatment, and she expressed how displeased she was about that order. She stated she had been through court-ordered treatment for years, and nothing helped. I told her to pick one thing that she wanted to change, not what anyone else told her to change, but what she wanted to change. I explained it could be something very different from what the court ordered her to change. She looked surprised and stated that no one had ever given her that option before. She said she wanted to work on the SDB of having a dirty kitchen counter. She added that she did not want to do anything else, just keep her kitchen counter clean. I said that would be fine. After two weeks, she arrived in my office with a big smile. She said she liked the way her counter looked so much that she cleaned the kitchen floor, and she liked that so much that she cleaned the rest of the kitchen. The child welfare worker asked what I was doing, because the woman had been in danger of losing her children for some time and had never had a clean kitchen until now. By the end of six weeks, the client said her marriage was much better and her husband no longer threatened to leave her. In addition, she said she was no longer in danger of losing her children. The child welfare worker verified that her children were no longer in danger of being removed from the home due to neglect and that the house was spotless. A year later, all was still well with both the marriage and the care of the house and children.

Getting Started Is Easy

It is time to start improving your life. Step one is to pick only one self-defeating behavior that you want to eliminate, but make it the one behavior, thought, or feeling you want most to change. It is important to choose something that you want to change, not something someone else told you to change. For children, have them choose the one thing they want to change, not something you or anyone else told them to change.

(Note: Bold text indicates an instruction to you. Do not read that part to the children. Either explain the material or do the demonstration. These can also serve as instructions for an adult who cannot read or write.)

[Next, for children, explain that they can change any behavior they want to change and that it is possible to change any behavior they do not like or any feeling they do not want to have. Tell them that they are in charge of how they think, feel, and act. You can use the camping and ele-

vator examples, as well as any examples appropriate for their age group, to show that how they choose their thoughts determines their feelings, which, in turn, determine their actions. You can use an example of a broken TV. They could choose to think, *I am missing my favorite TV show.* Based on that thought, they could choose to feel anger or sadness, and then from those feelings they could choose to throw a tantrum, cry, scream, pout, sulk, or any number of other choices. They could also choose to decide, *Wow, this is a chance to play games with my family!, I guess it is time to play outside,* or some other happy thought. These thoughts allow them to choose to feel happy, calm, or peaceful. Their actions would be to play games or run outside, or help mom with dinner, etc.

Another situation children seem to understand is when the teacher calls on them in class. Ask them to imagine being called on in class. Choices for what they think could range from *Wow! Now I can show off what I know!* to *Oh, no, why did she call on me? I want to hide under the desk.* Based on their choice of thoughts, they could feel either happy or horrified. Their actions could range from giving the correct answer, resulting in increased self-esteem, to sulking the rest of the day, or perhaps even running out of class crying.

All instructions that follow have been written in the voice of the person working on eliminating the self-defeating behavior. For children, either explain or read the instructions.]

How does an SDB get started? At one time, the behavior was helpful to you. It may have gotten you out of a bad situation, made you feel more at ease, or helped you get a friend. Now it is just dragging you down. An example of this is the snowball story that my former professor, Dr. Jonathon Chamberlain, used to tell.

[It helps to have the person working on the behavior hold a small garbage can during the story.]

It goes as follows: Let us say you are four-years-old and your mom asks you to take out the garbage. When you are four-years-old, that is a cool thing, and you feel important being able to do this job. It has been snowing outside, and the snow is a couple of feet deep on the ground. You take out the garbage and empty it into the main can outside. You feel important. Then you notice the bullies. They are very big, maybe ten-years-old. They are throwing snowballs at you! What are you going to do to protect yourself? Will you block the snowballs with the garbage can or catch them with the garbage can? Let us say that whatever you tried worked. You were not hit with a single snowball.

When you go back inside, your mom says, "Thank you for taking out the garbage! You did a great job." She then tries to take the garbage can from you. You say, "No!" and hang onto it because, after all, the bullies might follow you back into the house to throw snowballs at you, and you might need the garbage can for protection. If you are four-years-old, you might think like that. Then, that night, you take the garbage can to bed with you because, after all, the bullies might sneak into the house, just to throw snowballs at you while you are in bed. (Now, when I heard this part of the story, at first I thought, *even a four-year-old would not think like that.* Then I remembered reading a letter from my parents to my grandparents that was written when I was four-years-old and living in Germany. It described how I had sneaked outside, gotten snowballs, and thrown them at my parents when they were in bed.) Okay, four-year-olds would think like that. The behavior is still reasonable.

Now it is July, and the temperature is over a hundred degrees outside, and you are still carrying that garbage can because, after all, those bullies might have put snowballs in the freezer, just to throw at you in July. (When I heard this part of the story, I thought that no child would think that way. Then, I remembered one day during our first winter in Utah, I came home from class, and noticing there were snowballs in the freezer, asked my children why they had placed them there. They answered, "We want to throw them in the summer.") Yes, children do think that way. From a child's point of view, it is still reasonable to be carrying the garbage can in July.

Now, let us say you are in the first grade, and you are still carrying that garbage can around with you. The teacher asks you why you carry the garbage can everywhere. You have now been carrying that garbage can around for two years. What are you going to say to her? How will you feel? You will likely make up a reasonable excuse. If she tries to take it from you, you are not going to want to give it up and will try to hang onto it.

Now, you are an adult. You are working as a firefighter and still carrying the garbage can. The chief calls you into his office and asks why you are carrying the garbage can. By now, you have forgotten about the bullies and the reason you had started carrying the garbage can. The likelihood you would be afraid of ten-year-olds throwing snowballs at you is not big, particularly in a firehouse or at a fire. What are you going to tell the chief? You will likely make up a good excuse, such as you need to pick up the trash after the fire. How would you feel if he said you could not carry it around anymore? You have been carrying it all these years. You are not going to want to give it up. It is your security blanket.

Self-defeating behaviors are like the garbage can in the story. At one time, they were useful. Now they are just dragging you down. Some of us have many garbage cans weighing us down. Others have just a few. We can get rid of those garbage cans one by one.

An easy way to start eliminating your garbage cans is to use a paper garbage can. A template to make your garbage can is in this book. Tape the sides together. It should be small enough to fit in your pocket. (If you fill one paper garbage can, then make another and carry both of them, and so on.) Cut out little slips of paper that read: *I chose to do my SDB. I can choose not to do it.* You may also use plain strips of paper and just say the words to yourself as you put them into the garbage can. You need to watch yourself for when you do your SDB, and each time you choose to do it, you take one of the slips of paper, read it, and put it into your garbage can. This will help you catch yourself doing it and keep track. It will also reinforce the idea that you choose to do it and can choose not to do it. Be certain to carry the garbage can or cans and the slips everywhere you go.

Another part of step one is to put a penny or a pebble in your shoe. Every time you feel the object, say to yourself—with feeling—*I choose to...*and then say the opposite of your SDB. For instance, if your SDB is nail biting, say, *I choose to have beautiful nails.* If your SDB is controlling your anger, you could say, *I choose to remain calm and in control.* If your SDB is breaking your diet, you could say to yourself, *I choose to be slender* or *I choose to eat healthy.*

The third part of step one is to shout the cheers listed below with feeling, at least two times a day—more often if time and circumstances permit. It may feel funny at first, but the cheers actually help.

[If a child is the one working on the SDB, it would help if a parent and siblings also participated in the cheers.]

Do these at the beginning and end of each day with great enthusiasm. It may feel funny at first, but it works. Think of yourself as a cheerleader who needs to be heard at the top of a huge stadium.

1. *How do I choose to feel?* Then answer: *I choose to feel happy, healthy, and fantastic!* (Punch the air while answering.)

2. *Who is the greatest person in the world?* Answer: *I am!* (Punch the air while answering.)

3. *One, two, three, four, SDBs are gone for sure!* (Do it while clapping in time, and repeat it four times, each time saying it faster than the last.) Then shout, *Charge!* and punch the air once.

4. *What do I do when faced with a problem?* Answer: *Solve it!* (Punch air while answering.)

5. *Where do I smash my SDBs?* Answer: *Upstairs, downstairs, all around the neighborhood.* (Reach up, then down, then spread your arms out wide.) Repeat four times.

6. *What do we do with SDBs?* Answer: *Smash 'em, bash 'em, beat 'em into the ground!* (Make a fist and beat the air in time like a drum.)

7. *Who do I choose to love?* Answer: *Everyone!* (Punch the air while answering.)

8. *Who's going to smash their SDBs?* Answer: *I am!* (Punch the air while answering.)

End by applauding yourself! Cheer for yourself!

If you're doing cheers with more than one person, you can add the following: *How are we in this?* Answer: *Together!* (Punch the air while answering.)

These activities alone have been enough to eliminate self-defeating behaviors. Continue these activities throughout the entire six-week program.

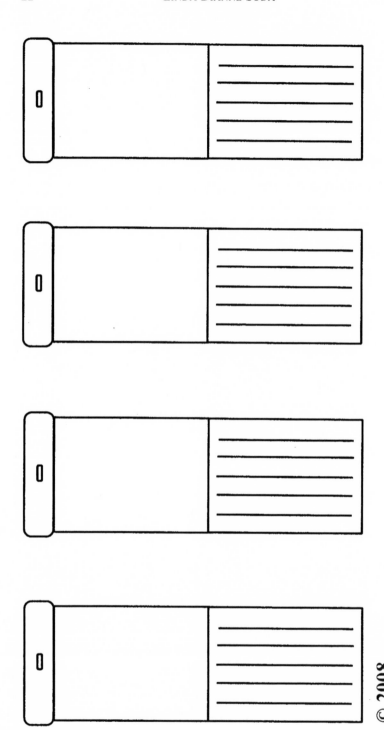

© 2008

Cut out and fold at the center line then tape the sides. Then fold over top flap for a lid.

I chose to do my SDB. I can choose not to do it.

I chose to do my SDB. I can choose not to do it.

I chose to do my SDB. I can choose not to do it.

I chose to do my SDB. I can choose not to do it.

I chose to do my SDB. I can choose not to do it.

I chose to do my SDB. I can choose not to do it.

I chose to do my SDB. I can choose not to do it.

I chose to do my SDB. I can choose not to do it.

I chose to do my SDB. I can choose not to do it.

I chose to do my SDB. I can choose not to do it.

I chose to do my SDB. I can choose not to do it.

I chose to do my SDB. I can choose not to do it.

I chose to do my SDB. I can choose not to do it.

I chose to do my SDB. I can choose not to do it.

I chose to do my SDB. I can choose not to do it.

I chose to do my SDB. I can choose not to do it.

I chose to do my SDB. I can choose not to do it.

I chose to do my SDB. I can choose not to do it.

I chose to do my SDB. I can choose not to do it

The Next Step Is a Piece of Cake

Each step should be started at least a week after starting the previous step, and you should continue doing each step's tasks as you add a new step. Step two involves techniques or how you do your SDB.

Now you may be saying to yourself, *I don't do it. It just happens.* I will tell you a true story that my wonderful former professor, Dr. Jonathon Chamberlain, told about how a woman did her SDB. The woman's SDB was that she ate a chocolate cake every day. Her husband told her, "No more chocolate cake." She said she would not eat any more, but she continued to eat a chocolate cake every day. Dr. Chamberlain said this is how she did her SDB. Every day she would say goodbye to her husband and kiss him on the cheek. She waved to him as he left and had good intentions of not eating any more chocolate cake that day.

Then about an hour after he left, she would ask herself, *What if company comes over? What do I have to serve them?* She rarely had company stop by, but that did not stop her from doing her SDB. Next, she said to herself, *I know. I will make a chocolate cake.*

She went to the pantry and got out the flour, sugar, and chocolate. She got out the bowl, mixer, spatula, and pans. She went to the refrigerator and got out the milk and eggs. She got her recipe book, opened it to the well-used page, and followed each step carefully. She measured and added the ingredients, each in the right order. She preheated the oven, poured the batter into the pans, put the pans in the oven, and set the timer. Then she washed the bowl, mixer, and spatula, along with all the other utensils she had used. She put away the flour, sugar, and other ingredients and then turned the page to her favorite frosting recipe. She got each ingredient out for the frosting, got the measuring utensils and bowl out, measured each ingredient, and added it in the bowl. Then she mixed them all together. When the timer went off, she pulled the cake out of the oven and let it cool. She put the bottom layer on a cake plate, picked up the spatula to frost it, dipped the spatula in the frosting, lifted the spatula to the cake, dipped the spatula in the frosting, and spread it repeatedly until the cake was finished. Then she washed the dishes, wiped the counter, and put all the ingredients away, along with everything else she had used to make the frosting. She put the cake on the kitchen table, went into the living room, and sat down.

She thought, *What if the cake isn't any good?* (Now, how many times would a chocolate cake not be good?) Then she said to herself, *Maybe I should test a piece, just to see if it is any good.* The woman then walked into the kitchen. She walked to the cupboard and pulled out a plate. Next she went to the drawer, pulled out a knife and fork, lifted the knife to the cake, cut a piece, put it on the plate, put the fork near the cake, then cut a piece with the fork, put the fork to her mouth, put the piece of cake in her mouth, chewed it, and swallowed it. Then she repeated the process until she finished the piece of cake. She washed the knife, fork, and plate. The woman sat back down and thought to herself, *What if that was the only good piece in the cake? I had better try a piece from the other side.* She walked back to the cake, cut a slice, put it on the plate, and put the fork to the piece, and cut off a bite's worth, picked it up with the fork, put the piece to her mouth, put it in her mouth, chewed it, and swallowed it. The woman then repeated the process until that piece was finished.

She sat for a short while and then said to herself, *Hmmm, what if those were the only two good pieces in the whole cake? I would be mortified if company came and I gave them cake that did not taste good!* She walked to the kitchen and repeated the process. This time she chose a piece from another quadrant of the cake. It was then almost noon, and no company had come yet. She thought to herself, *Maybe those were the only good pieces in the cake. It would be horrible if someone came over and I served a bad piece of cake.* She repeated the process systematically and ate one more piece of cake. She sat down for a while again. There was still no company. Finally, she realized her husband would be home soon and would discover she had eaten cake again—four whole pieces of it. She panicked. She went to the kitchen and finished the cake, one bite at a time, then washed the dishes and put them away to hide the evidence. By the time her husband came home, she had again eaten an entire chocolate cake that day.

She could have stopped doing her SDB before any of the steps. What steps were involved in doing her SDB? There were quite a few—try counting them. There were hundreds of steps, from what she told herself, to each step in making the cake, to each movement in eating the cake, and cleaning up afterwards. If there were thirty-five steps to the kitchen and thirty-five steps back, and she went there multiple times, the steps would add up. Count how many steps she could have made while in the kitchen. If we assume only ten steps each time she walked from one place to another while in the kitchen, that will add up. Add up how many strokes it would take to frost a cake. How many movements involved in dipping the spreader into the frosting and then to the cake to frost it. Add in how many different movements involved in getting ingredients from the cupboard and getting mixing and measuring tools from the drawer or cupboard, mixing, pouring, setting the timer, removing the cake from a pan and putting it on a cake plate, cutting the cake, and even placing a piece on the plate. Then add in how many movements it would take to take a bite of cake. She needed to pick up a fork, move her hand to the cake, cut the piece, put it on the fork, move the piece to her mouth, open her mouth, put the piece of cake inside her mouth, remove the fork, chew it however many times necessary, and then swallow it. Each chew and swallow counts as a step because at any time prior to swallowing she could spit out the piece of cake, and stop. Then she repeated this as many times as it took to finish the piece. Multiply the number of steps involved for the cutting and eating of the cake, by the number of times she cut and ate a piece. Then add in the number of steps involved in cleaning up and washing the dishes using this same method of counting movements and actual steps. Add in the number of thoughts involved. It adds up to literally hundreds of steps.

She could stop at any time prior to finishing the cake. The earlier she stopped, the easier it would be. If she chewed the piece twice and stopped, then spit it out, and put the rest of the cake away or threw it away, she would stop the behavior at that point. Even if she caught herself after one piece, and either threw away, put away, or gave away the rest of the cake, she would be improving. It would be easier to catch herself the next time she chose to start doing her SDB. Her self-esteem would also likely improve, as she saw she was able to stop.

What are all the steps you do in order to do your SDB? If your SDB is nail biting, what are all the steps or techniques you use to do nail biting? Stop and think. Do you tell yourself something without thinking first, such as, *I always feel uncomfortable in crowds, I may not make a friend,* or *No one likes me?* What do you tell yourself without thinking? To give herself permission to do her SDB, the woman in the cake story used the thoughts that company might come. Next, what feelings do you have based on the thoughts? Do you feel anxious? Do you feel angry? Now, what behaviors or actions are involved? You need to lift your hand to your face, get your fingers in position, open your mouth, reposition your fingers to bite the nails, then bite down, many times, (each bite is a step) swallow the piece or spit out the piece, moving your fingers and mouth as you do the behavior.

The woman in the chocolate cake story could have stopped at any point before she ate the cake. The best and easiest place to stop was in the thought process, where she thought to herself that company might come and she would have nothing to give them. If she did not stop there, she could have stopped as she walked to the kitchen and turned around instead. She could have stopped while getting the ingredients together or while taking the pans out of the cupboard. She even could have stopped as late as putting the piece into her mouth. The earlier she stopped herself, the easier it would be to stop, but stopping was still possible anywhere along the way.

If, for example, your SDB is nail biting, the easiest place to stop is with the thought. You can stop anywhere along the way, including right up to the point you start biting down on the nail, but it is easiest if you stop at the thought or before you do anything.

If you have anger control issues, the best place to stop doing your SDB would be with the thoughts. You could stop anywhere before the behaviors were completed, but it is much easier to stop with the thoughts. If you change your thoughts, your feelings and behaviors will change. Just as in the story of the elevator, where your foot was stomped on, when the thoughts changed, even though you were still in pain, the feelings changed and the behavior changed.

In step two, you write on paper all the ways you do your SDB.

[If you are reading this to someone who cannot read or write, have them draw pictures of all the ways they do their SDB.]

Start with the thoughts. For example, *He cut in front of me.* Then add the feelings and each step of the behaviors.

[If you are able to read and write well enough, make a list of all the ways you do your SDB, starting with the thoughts, and describe each step along the way, until you have done the SDB. Next, write the opposite of each step in doing your SDB. (This is doing your Best-Self Behaviors or being your Best Self.) One way to do this is to divide the paper in half with a vertical line. On one side of the paper, write the SDB steps, and on the other side, write the Best-Self steps, which correspond but are the opposite of the SDB steps. For those unable to write, have them draw a picture of the opposite of each of the steps of the SDB and describe them to someone else.]

When you have written down all the steps or techniques in doing your SDB, try to catch yourself as early as possible in the steps to doing your SDB. Switch to the opposite of the SDB action. For example, if you were working on anger management, and you said to yourself, *He cut in front of me.*, you would try to catch yourself at this point in the process and say to yourself, *My, he is in a hurry. I choose to see this as a chance for me to develop patience.*

In the case of the woman who ate an entire chocolate cake every day, instead of asking herself what she could serve unexpected company, she could choose one of several options. One option might be, *What if company comes? They haven't come unannounced in a while, but if they do come, they will be happy with the ice water I just put in the refrigerator or maybe some fresh vegetables or fresh fruit I can cut up. Of course, if they come unannounced, they are coming to see me, not to eat. A glass of water, milk, or juice might be all that I need to offer.*

Think about what you choose to do to enact your SDB, and then figure out the opposite and do that. It usually takes about two weeks to change a behavior. Those two weeks will require effort. After that, it is usually easier.

[At this point in the workshop or classroom setting, I usually do what I call my *magic-oven* routine. With children, this is especially fun, but even adults get into the spirit of this. I have two long cardboard file drawers or big boxes (big enough for two or more pans) that I have covered with paper and marked to make them look like ovens. I have a large apron, two large mixing bowls, large mixing spoons, two empty cake pans, potholders, many small strips of paper, and a pen. I ask class members to raise their hands and offer ingredients in any SDB. One volunteer is the chef and wears the chef's apron, and either the chef or I write down on the paper strips whatever suggestions the class makes for ingredients in an SDB. It can be just a word or even a little picture. I ask how much of that ingredient we should add—a cup, one-fourth cup, a tablespoon, tea-spoon, and so on. I accept whatever suggestions for amounts that they give, even if the suggestion is a gallon or a truckload, and I have the chef add it to the mixing bowl. When we have enough ingredients added, I have the chef thoroughly mix the strips of papers—or ingredients—with a spoon. I make sure the chef knows, along with the rest of those participating, how important it is to mix the ingredients well. I then have the chef pretend to grease a pan and pour all the ingredients into it. I tell the chef to scrape the

contents of the bowl into the pan so we will not miss any of the ingredients. Then I pretend to turn on the oven, and I ask what temperature we should cook this mixture. I always go with the temperature that is most offered. I personally put the pan with the SDB ingredients in it into the SDB oven. I either have an oven timer with a bell or pretend to have one. I then either set or pretend to set the timer and wait a minute. Either the oven timer rings or I just say, "Ding!" I then use the potholders, open the magic oven, and, from the back, pull out a pan that I had put in the oven before leaving my home or office. In *this* pan is a mud pie concoction with dirt, stones, twigs, and sometimes little pieces of garbage. I then say enthusiastically, "This is the SDB we baked." Next, I ask who would like a piece of it. In ninety-nine percent of the classes, no one wants a piece. To the other one percent, I just grin and say, "I will be happy to serve it up later, on the condition that you do not want what we are about to make with the Best-Self ingredients."

I then have the chef use a fresh bowl and mixing spoon, and we follow the same procedure, but have everyone suggest ingredients and the amounts that would go into being a Best Self. I have the chef mix it, making sure everyone participating knows how important it is to mix it well and smooth out any lumps. I again pretend to set the temperature, and after the chef greases the pan and puts the ingredients into it, scraping the bowl carefully, I put it in the Best-Self oven. Again, I time it, and after the ding sounds, get the potholders and use them to pull out a pan from the Best-Self oven, one that I placed in the oven before class. I have had various yummy goodies in that pan, and I usually have the Best-Self pan multiply into several pans with goodies such as cupcakes, candy, and brownies, enough for everyone participating. They are always ready to eat, complete with frosting if required. I then ask if anyone wants to enjoy the results of being their Best Self by having

some of what came out of the oven. I have yet to have anyone turn this down, unless they were sugar-restricted, and,
in that case, I have some sugar-free treat emerge for them.]

Before they receive the treat, I ask all partaking if they
agree they would rather have the Best Self than the SDB.
This exercise usually makes the point: You get the results
of what you put into your efforts.]

Minimizing and Disowning

We all minimize and disown our SDBs. What are minimizing and disowning? They are the ways you say each time you do your SDB, "It is not so bad" and "It is not my fault." Another way we do this is by saying, "If she hadn't said that, I would not have done…" Still other ways we minimize and disown are by rationalizing: "Everyone is doing it," "Just this once won't hurt," and "No one will ever notice." Remember the excuses you used for carrying a garbage can when you were grown up. You originally had used it just to protect yourself from bullies.

Minimizing and disowning are similar. They are the excuses we use to keep doing our SDB. Some other examples are:

- "If I go five miles over the speed limit, it is all right because everyone else does."

- "The stores plan for 'shrinkage,' so it is okay to take this little thing."
- "So what if I stretch the truth when talking about my neighbor? It makes the story more interesting."
- "It is Joey's fault I hit him."
- "Looking at someone else's paper during a test is not cheating. Besides, I would have come up with that answer, anyway."
- "It is not risky. It is exciting."
- "It is okay to do this because someone dared me."
- "It is my spouse's fault that I…" (You can finish the sentence.)

What are the ways you minimize or disown your SDB?

[If the person cannot write, have them draw pictures. If they can write, list them.]

Step four is to note each time you minimize or disown your SDB. Add slips of paper to your garbage can as you do when you do your SDB, as this is part of your SDB.

[When I arrive at this point in a workshop or classroom setting, I usually call a volunteer up to the front. I have an oversized chain, heavy enough to pull a truck if needed and long enough to wrap around a person at least a few times. I have the group list all the steps in doing their SDB, all the ways they minimize and disown, and all the prices involved. For each of the ways, I go up one link on the chain, until I have finished all the links. I then wrap the chain around the volunteer, demonstrating how you are weighed down by the chains of your SDB and are handicapped by it in various ways. To demonstrate how you are handicapped by it, the volunteer needs to stand on one leg. I then direct the volunteer to move around the room to get to work or school, pick up the children from the sitter, do grocery shopping, play with friends, do his chores, and so forth. The volunteer must get around the room on one leg with the chains

wrapped around him. The rule is that he must keep doing one thing after another, in this manner, until he says he is ready to give up his SDB. At this point, he gets to take off the chains and walk on both feet again. I have everyone applaud. It is a good kinetic or physical way to demonstrate just how much our SDBs weigh us down and handicap us. Even the hardiest children eventually get tired and decide to get rid of their SDB at this demonstration so that they can sit down.]

Prices We Pay

Just as in the magic oven illustration, if you put in SDB ingredients, you will get SDB results. If you do SDB behaviors, you will pay the prices for those behaviors. Remember, you can stop anywhere along the way before doing the SDB, but it is harder the farther you go. One thing that can help before you do your SDB is if you remember the prices you will pay before you have to pay them.

If a bank robber thought about jail, dishonor, missing years of life, maybe being shot, losing family and friends—would he be thinking it would be great to rob a bank? No. What is he thinking as he plans the robbery? He is thinking easy money, fun spending it, no work for the money. If you think about your SDB prices before you do the behavior, will you be as likely to want to do it? If the woman who worked on the SDB of eating a chocolate cake every day thought about an increasing waistline, getting a spouse angry, not fitting into clothes, getting on the scale, how much less likely would she want to indulge, compared to thinking only about the yummy taste? If you are working on biting your nails and are thinking about how awful they look bitten, and how sick it can make you to put all those germs on your fingers in your mouth, and how it hurts when they bleed, are you more or less likely to bite them?

At the end of this chapter, I created a page of price tags. Use one tag for each price you pay. You can make additional price tags for your own use if needed.

[If the person cannot write, have that person draw a picture of each price.]

Step four is to carry the price tags with you and read them several times a day. Make sure you also read them each time you do your SDB. It will keep the prices in the forefront of your consciousness. In other words, you will be thinking about the prices before you have to pay them. That way, you can avoid doing what would cause you to need to pay them. If you think of more prices as you go along, just write or draw more price tags. Carry them with you and look at them, too. Continue these activities throughout the remainder of the six-week program.

Price Tags
(The actual Prices paid for my SDB)
One tag for each price (children can draw a picture of the price on the tag)

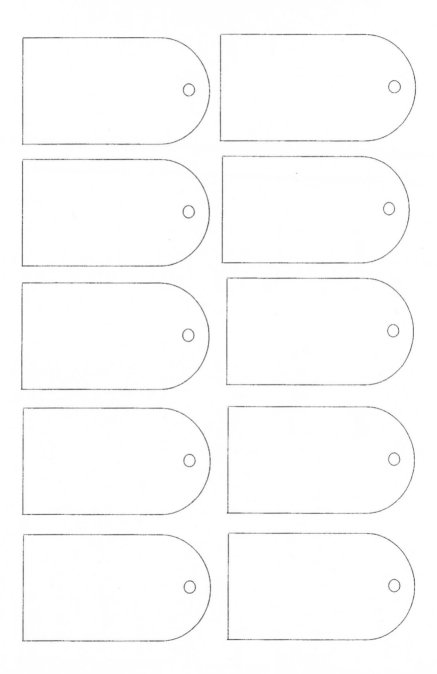

Fears

After working your way through all the previous steps, if you are still doing your SDB, the chances are you are afraid to stop doing it. *That is silly,* you may be thinking. *I want to get rid of my SDB.* I am sure you do want to get rid of it, but you are just afraid of what will happen when you do. Do you remember the garbage can story? The little child was afraid of snowballs hitting him, so he hung onto the garbage can. That is what is happening to you.

I want you to pretend you are in a jungle. All of a sudden, you see a tiger chasing you. You run. Just as you are about to be caught and eaten, you see a very thin tree, right by the edge of a tall cliff. You climb the tree. Because the tiger is so big, and you are not nearly as big, you are able to climb to the top of the tree. The tiger cannot follow you up the tree. You are safe. The tiger circles around you for a while, waiting for you to come down, but you do not.

Finally, as night falls, the tiger gives up and goes on to other prey. You stay in the tree that saved your life because the tiger might come back. The next morning, the tiger has not returned, but you are still in the tree, just in case he shows up. There is no tiger in sight for a full day more, but you are still in the tree. It saved your life. Suddenly, a strong wind comes up. The tree was already slightly bending because of your weight, and now begins to crack just at the bottom and bends toward the cliff. If you do not let go, you will go over the cliff with the tree. You still hang on to the tree for dear life. After all, that tree saved your life. The tree starts to fall over the cliff. Still, you hang on to it because it saved your life once. Down, **down**, you go, down the steep cliff. As you go down the cliff, you **notice** a ledge. You could grasp it on your way down and pull **your**self in, but it would mean letting go of the tree. You do **not want** to let go of the tree. It saved your life. You think, *If I let go of the tree, I will be eaten by the tiger.* What will you choose to do?

On the other side of your fears are good things. You just cannot see them. It is like having to go through a cloud or fog, and on the other side is everything wonderful that you ever dreamed. You just cannot see it. You have to get past your fears to get to it, because there is the "What if..." You can see the prices you pay for doing your SDB. You know they are bad and harmful, but at least you know what they are. You do not know what it would be like not to have the bad. For example, you might think, *If I did not do my SDB, no one would like me.* Another thought might be, *If I stopped doing my SDB, I would not be able to do my job as well.* If your SDB was procrastination, which is the SDB often associated with the SDB of perfectionism, your fear might be, *If I finish this or finish on time, I will fail, or it will not be perfect.* Perhaps you are saying to yourself, *I don't know what it would be like, but at least I know what staying the same is like.*

[If the person cannot write, have them draw pictures of what is scary to them if they do not do their SDB anymore. With small children, drawing anything that scares them is effective.]

Little cloud pictures are printed at the end of this chapter. There should be enough for all your fears, but, if not, please make more for your own use. Be sure to list all your fears, by either drawing or writing them. When you finish, put a mark by all those fears that are fantasy, or not likely to ever happen. Put a different mark by those that are real fears, or things that could happen. For the fears that are real, write down or draw ways to avoid that or prevent that from happening. This could be such as looking both ways before crossing the street, or crossing only at cross walks. Examples of real vs. fantasy fears are fear of being attacked by a dragon in New York City—fantasy. Fear of being hit by a car [For an SDB of being afraid to cross the street]—real. If your SDB was fear of swimming, then fear of drowning is real. On the other hand, if your SDB was fear of elevators, fear of drowning is fantasy. It is not likely that you will drown when you are in an elevator, unless there is really bad plumbing or a really huge tidal wave. It is less likely you will drown or be hit by a car if you take precautions. If your SDB was holding a garbage can, and you are now an adult firefighter, and your fear is that bullies will throw snowballs at you, is that fantasy or real? If fourth-grade bullies throw snowballs at you while you are fighting a fire, how big of a problem is that?

[In my workshops, I do a roadmap exercise as a demonstration at this point. I have included the basic map diagram at the end of this chapter. I usually station participants at each stop, holding a sign that indicates what is at that stop. As the participant passes a stop, I have the one holding the sign say what is on their sign. With minimizing and disowning, I have them say *It is not SO bad* and *it is not MY fault.* When there are not enough participants, I simply place signs with the various steps along the road. In that case, as the person passes the signs I say what is on the sign. I also have someone standing in front of a sheet that blocks the view of what is behind it, holding a sign with a cloud that has the word *Fears* written in scary letters. This person pretends to be frightening. A sign that says Best Self is visible on or above the sheet. The road is set up like a V, and the other players start at the bottom of the V-shaped road. Along one road route, they will encounter Techniques, Minimizing and Disowning, Prices, and then, adjoining Prices, is SDB Jail. The other half of the V-shaped road has a scary-looking person with a sign marked *Fears,* and it is straight until you hit the end. The scary person in front of the sheet is at the end, but a sign saying Best Self is visible on the top of the sheet. Players can change direction at any time before they pay the prices and wind up in SDB jail. (However, they have to go back to the starting point if they chose to change direction.) When they are in SDB jail, they must stay for a turn or two, and then they may start over from the beginning and choose again. I usually give the participants some play money to use to pay the prices when they land in SDB jail. If they choose the straight-and-narrow path to Fears and get past the scary-looking person, who usually tries to scare them into not passing, they can go behind the sheet. I ask them to call out to others, from behind the sheet, whether it is a good idea to get past their fears. They always say it is. On the other side of the sheet is an assortment of treats. They may keep the play money or trade it for treats, or sometimes I have them keep the play money and enjoy the treats. Eventually, everyone will choose to get past his fears in this demonstration.]

FEARS
write or draw a picture of the fears you choose to use to stop you from eliminating
your SDB and whether mythical or real — one fear cloud for each fear

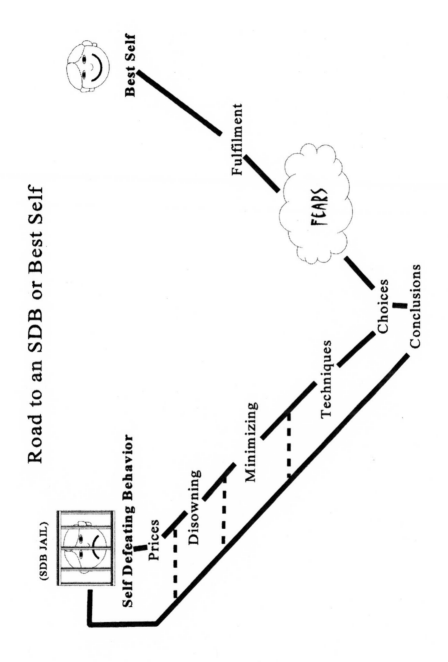

Road to an SDB or Best Self

Picture in Your Mind

The final step—guided imagery.

[If there is no tape or CD with this book, you can easily make your own tape, or have a friend read you the imagery in a soft tone of voice. All the words and instructions are below.]

Get into a comfortable position, and get as relaxed as possible. Now breathe in through your nose and out through your mouth, using deep breaths. Have the air go into your stomach or diaphragm. As you breathe out, whisper the word *relax,* slowly. Do this several times.

[Wait a minute before going on with the reading.]

Now picture yourself on a beautiful path going toward whatever you want most in the whole world.

[Wait a couple of minutes before starting again.]

Now, notice something is blocking you. It will not let you by. Fight it. Do whatever is necessary to win.

[Wait a minute or two.]

Totally destroy the obstacle in whatever way you can.

[Wait a couple of minutes.]

Next, go back down that beautiful path to whatever you want most. Notice all the beauty on the path. Feel how good it is to walk on the path. Notice a gentle breeze. Enjoy the feeling.

[Wait a few minutes.]

Suddenly, a huge wall appears blocking your path. You cannot go under or around it, and you cannot climb over it. Find a way to get to the other side, where you can be your Best Self and have what you really want in life.

[Wait a few minutes.]

When you are on the other side, destroy the wall. Do not leave a single trace of it.

[Wait a few minutes.]

Now look around you. Enjoy the beauty. Feel the joy of being there. Picture yourself going through each day as your Best Self, making all the right choices. Enjoy the feeling. Feel the joy.

[Wait several minutes.]

When you are ready, open your eyes.

Write down what you saw and felt, or draw a picture of it. Each morning as you awaken, picture yourself going through each day as your Best Self for the rest of your life.

Congratulations! You have graduated! You have completed all of the steps.

- You caught yourself doing your SDB, put a piece of paper in a paper garbage can each time you did your SDB and said, "I chose to do my SDB. I can choose not to do it."
- You put a penny or a pebble in your shoe and each time you felt it, you said to yourself, "I choose to…" and said the opposite of your SDB.

- You did your cheers (affirmations) at least twice a day.
- You wrote or drew all the steps you did to do your SDB (or the ingredients in your SDB) and the opposite of them.
- You wrote or drew all the ways you minimized or disowned your SDB and learned how it weighed you down.
- You wrote or drew (in little price tags) all the prices you paid for doing your SDB and read them several times a day and each time you did your SDB.
- You wrote or drew (in little clouds) your fears about eliminating your SDB, and realized what is a real fear versus what is a mythical fear, then figured out how to approach real fears, and realized that if you got past your fears and eliminated your SDB good things were on the other side of the unknown.
- You did the "picture in your mind' exercise. Each morning you now picture going through your day without your SDB.
- You are now empowered to eliminate any SDB that you desire to eliminate. You are in control of your thoughts, feelings, and behaviors. You can re-do the steps at any time in the future for any SDB. You are the greatest!

Certificate of Achievement

In recognition of excellence in eliminating self-defeating behaviors,

Your name

Is empowered to eliminate any self-defeating behavior for the rest of his/her life and is a Best Self Superhero.

Signed: *Linda Dianne Suda, M.Ed., L.P.C.*

Printed in the United States
151537LV00004B/59/P

9 781606 939741